Solitary
Solitude
Sanctuary

Carol Alena Aronoff, Ph.D.

www.StoneCompassPress.com

10 9 8 7 6 5 4 3 2 1

For those in solitary confinement or in prisons of the mind, may you find solace and awaken to your true nature.

PREFACE

This poetry collection was conceived several years ago after listening to a public radio interview on juveniles in solitary confinement. I was so appalled by the terrible, lasting effects of this inhumane, soul-destroying punishment that I decided to research it further. I recalled similar actions taken with patients on psychiatric wards in VA hospitals where I did my postgraduate psychology internship in the 1960's as well as the isolating effects of mental illness I saw while living and working in a therapeutic commune in London based on the approach of psychiatrists, R.D. Laing and David Cooper. Soon, the heart of the topic began to take on larger meaning and I felt called to write about all aspects of solitary: confinement, mental illness, quarantine, chosen pursuits and careers, solitude, spiritual retreat and finding sanctuary. The writing of these poems was a journey, partly into the past, with the hope of bringing more compassion and understanding to the present and future.

CONTENTS

1 SUSPENDED IN AMBER

Letter to a Prisoner in Solitary

I need to tell you right away—
I've never been to prison,
not even as a visitor
though I lost my son behind bars
to loneliness and neglect.
I have no idea what it's like
to spend whole days, weeks,
years suspended in amber like
an insect under glass or fish
in a small, solitary bowl waiting
for the few flakes of food,
hour of caged exercise,
the once-a-week shower
that never leaves you
feeling clean.

Still, I feel impelled to write
you and hope this letter
is slipped through the slot as
companion to your evening
meal. Does mail help you
feel less alone? Does it matter
that you don't know the sender?
That it leaves your imagination
free to conjure up a caring sister,
worried mother, loving friend?
Does it make a difference? Perhaps
the paper itself, its thin body,
curved blue letters will be enough
for you to feel like you've
been touched.

A Poet in Solitary

Each place has its own perfume:
the tang of autumn leaves burning
in rural Vermont, of piñon and juniper
in high desert, the pungent potpourri
of belching fumes and curry in Delhi,
apples fermenting on the ground
in Wenatchee but this place– this place
has the stink of despair, of barely
suppressed violence, the unwashed
sweat of death, any sweetness or
subtle scents of peace lilies are left
outside barred windows and gates,
orphaned along with dreams of future
and family.

Within these punishing walls
of confinement, barren of any trace
of comfort or flowers of hope, this
drug-addled, cold turkey poet must
find a way to reconstitute a world,
at least in imagination and memory:
a world of small kindnesses and
beauty, where the spirit floats free
and all sounds are church bells
and jazzy percussion. The stainless
steel toilet/sink/drinking fountain has
taken on the glow of *The Thinker* under
moonlight and like Rodin, I sculpt
The Vanquished, seeking rebirth.

A Fifteen-Year-Old Asks, Is There an Ever After?

Before I did
something stupid,
landed in prison
and ended up in
solitary, I had a life.

Maybe not much
of one but still....
I was young, poor
yet full of swagger.
Thought I'd grow up

to be a rapper or
mechanic, drive
a cool car, have a
girlfriend with long
blond hair, a real house.

Pipe dreams all– after
I hit him with that bat
when he dissed my sister
and pulled a knife. He
wasn't supposed to die.

Now I sit on concrete–
tombstone for a living
death. Yet, still I dream
of an ever after where
I return to life.

A Child in Solitary

A windowless box the size of
a parking space   now home
A walk-in closet   with only a
bed sink and toilet No books
no paper or pens no nothing
Some days the walls   close in
and monsters hang   from the
ceiling   trigger a tidal wave
of terror   I am just thirteen
My crime   selling drugs
for   my   mom's boyfriend
talking back t o a nasty guard
I am living   my own funeral
Some days   I feel I no longer
exist I cut myself   to see my
blood write the word   help

No One Can See Me

Nothing   can penetrate
these pain-soaked   walls
Only smells   like locker
room sweat   toilet stink
mildew fear   and sounds
of torment   the chains
of convict shuffle drone of
fluorescent lighting   rants
and cursing   desperate
raving   jingling keys
that open   nothing

Discarded like trash   like
rotten food   at the back
of the fridge   disowned
by family community world
At sixteen I am growing up
unseen   unknown
in   a sterile coffin
all on my   own
with mice and   roaches
my   only   companions
and thoughts of   death

A Woman's View

I can do this, I thought
as they shoved me
in the cell, a cement
cauldron. I can dream
my way through, crochet
my soul threads near
a wall. I can deal with
the slab for a bed, thin
sheet, the slot for food.
In my mind, I will add
red cushions, thick
comforter, a picture of
Mary above my head.

Then I noticed the
all-in-one stainless
steel unit in the corner,
hideous marvel of
someone's nightmare.
Creepy silver demon
with open jaws and tail.
No decorator would
have thought this up.
No woman.

Where in nature do you
pee where you drink
or move your bowels
where you also wash?
Even sloths know this.
It will take more than
imagination to survive in
here, more than *que sera,
sera*. I regret the actions
that led me to this, offer
a prayer to stay human.

Safety in Silence

I weep without a whisper,
no gesture, no slightest
tremor to give me away.

Safety in silence, silent as a
swordfish in deep water, a soul
shrouding its light. Invisible.

Secret vow that must remain
secret in a barred house of
secrets. In my cell, a solitary

respite, place to grieve– awful
though it is. One day, I will find
the daughter I lost to drugs,

indifference. One day, I will
claim myself in lost baggage,
reclaim my sense of worth.

The crime that put me in the hole:
sticking up for someone in a fight;
my code of honor, red flag to guards

who see only dishonor. Regret lines
the walls of my cell, my tears weave
invisible tapestries spelling out hope.

A White Paper

The walls
white
almost blinding
stark
neon
sterile
not pure

No clock
to break
the whiteness
divide
the endless
into bearable
blocks or hint
at a future
beyond
these walls

I dream
of monthly blood
leaving tracks
on all this whiteness
marking passage
leaving a mark
a triumph
of matter over mind
over whiteness

Before solitary
I thought of white
as color
a summer scarf
a swan
I thought of hell
as red
as fire

Fighting Numbers
for Anthony Gay, former inmate, and the others

8,   0   0   0   days
192, 0   0   0   hours
11,520,   0   0   0 minutes

22   interminable   years
in   a cell   the size
of   his parents'   bed
enough   to drive   a sane man
up the walls   and out of his mind

Young unruly   stallion fighting for
his family's honor   stealing
another teen's hat   a single dollar
bill Awarded probation   then 3 1/2
years for driving   without a license
Brawling in prison   sealed
his future   spiraled out of control
into segregation   then endless
solitary   despair at no way out

Demons of dark   now haunting by
day   thoughts amplified like
skywriting   Panic written on blank
walls facing the abyss   Sinking
sinking   sinking   into
hopelessness rage   madness

A memory   of getting attention
and sympathy at 12   for downing
some pills   offers fleeting relief
and a path   to human contact
Slicing open   body parts
over and over   zipper   in his
scrotum   screw in his ear
brings momentary kindness   care
Makes him feel alive   Makes him
feel   Kind of like a drug addict
you have   to up   the ante

In Memory of Herman Wallace, One of the Angola 3

"I'm often asked what did I come to prison for; and now that I think about it…., It doesn't matter what I came here for, what matters now is what I leave with. And I can assure you, however I leave, I won't leave nothing behind."
—Herman Wallace

A man's history in three paces
from toilet to cell door The lie
that kept him locked away   for
40 years 23 hours   at a time
in the hole a near empty   box

Retaliation for speaking out for
shaping black bones and sinew
into a prowl of panthers against
inhumanity torture and slavery
Yassuh Angola where   officers

called Freemen   work   where
best behaved   black prisoners
known as Houseboys   wash
guards' cars   clean their houses
water   flowers

Where a prison warden ignored
the overturned convictions Kept
Herman Wallace in   solitary
feared blacks following after him
for his   radical   humane ideas

Not seen for decades by inmates
Illnesses ignored until gravely ill
a judge released him Liver cancer
claimed his life three days   later
I'm free he said   *I'm free, I'm free*

AKA Kinetic Justice

Blood fills   a darkened cell
trails into the corridor where
two half-dead prisoners one
mentally ill   the other trying
to help are beaten by guards
dragged unconscious   then
dumped   This oft repeated
Boschian nightmare   veiled
by clouds   of pepper spray
the coverup of brutal prison
personnel

What price   standing up for
Justice   for brothers behind
bars   52 months in solitary
for striking against   forced
prison labor   transfers to
notorious prisons   bogus
charges extortion   beatings
all to silence   Robert Earl
Council and break his spirit
AKA Kinetic Justice activist
and inspiration   unbending
ragged thorn   in corruption's
side

Forever Stamps

He was thrown into solitary
for having too many stamps.
Contraband, the guard said—
postage the prisoner wanted
for love letters to the sky,
odes to dirt, a postcard saying,
Wish I was there.

No pencils in the hole— could
be used as a weapon of self
destruction; so he wrote letters
in his head, painted them on
walls with food, recited them
to bare floor, grim ceiling.

There were days without words,
days he thought he must be
dying. And then in a rush, a few
sentences, a well-remembered
poem, a letter of forgiveness
to the prison warden that would
need no stamp.

Finding Paris

Her fans wanted nonstop glitter, a ditsy,
smiling sun to bathe them in confetti and
mirror balls— jeweled sunbeams reflecting
the love they craved, an unfillable hole.
The star amidst a starless night.

Beneath the well-crafted Mardi Gras mask,
a river of trauma: 20 hour stints in solitary
for hiding drugs she was forced to take, hidden
abuses, unhealed scars— no relief from expectations,
addicting adulation, drama. So many, famous

for being famous, sent to schools for discipline
with similar stories: Drew Barrymore, Paris Jackson….
Does rebellion, wild abandon, the search for
authenticity in a swamp of hungry ghosts justify
the crushing loss of freedom, damage to a soul?

Reading for Their Lives

Former prisoners have shared how
the written word saved their sanity
in solitary, encouraged them to dream,
even hope– for more than a life in limbo.

In isolation, books and letters: a lifeline.
One prisoner taught himself to read from
letters and a dictionary sent by a church
volunteer. Soon he fell in love with words,

wrote poems for convicts in exchange
for books. *Reading books became my line
of defense against the madness.**
Another prisoner still recalls the book

he read and re-read in the hole about a
brother and sister who became like family;
their story eased his loneliness and regret,
took him beyond unforgiving walls.

* Jimmy Santiago Baca, *A Place to Stand*

Solitary Art

In a Supermax prison,
fierce strokes, brush
wielded like anger's
mallet with paint thick
as congealed blood.
Blood spilled so many
years past still needing
release, redemption.

In a different prison,
a woman in solitary
allowed a small pen
and a few sheets of
paper, tools for survival,
lashes out in ink-drawn
fury, finds some relief
and a sense of control.

After thirty-three years
of a life sentence,
another inmate paints
on rocks found in the
prison yard; says, *No
matter where one
resides, beauty can
always be found.*

A Chance for Salvation
– For Jimmy: the last stanza

I am exiled, shunned by
those politely civilized
as well as by gatherings
of wolves.

Refugee
from impoverished
maps of misery
and hopelessness.

I am expatriate,
my motherland,
the one that birthed
and then betrayed me,

no longer my home.
No songs of redemption,
no longer
praying for escape.

I am tarnished,
debased
by my own reckoning,
my refusal to rise like wind,

to carry myself forward
past wannabe warriors
clustered like jackals
on street corners.

Instead, I give in
to their macho demands.
Easier to set aside dreams
than resist, risk early death.

Caught with gun, drugs, attitude
before I earn my colors, before
killing fills my resumé and brutality
freezes my blood.

Prison for the failed, an antidote for
me, retreat from worse alternatives
as long as I hang tough, make fear
a stranger; softness gets you killed

or worse, bravado puts me in the hole.
I sit resigned in empty dark when suddenly
the cell is filled with dazzling light. God appears
without my prayers: a chance for salvation

2 DOWN THE RABBIT HOLE

Detox in a CONEX Box   (Vietnam, 1971)

one hundred ten degrees   no windows   walls burning to the touch

one bucket   one blanket   one bottle of water

coming down   coming off   heroin

smack   China White   alone

bad dreams   corrugated metal nightmare   moaning

shakes   wrung out on barbed wire   crying out

dying   white phosphorous exploding   then silence

the hush   dead space   unclaimed

unburied   don't send me home   in pieces

VA Hospital Psych Ward, Circa 1960's

Aides held him down, they said
for his own good, pinned
a warning label on his striped
pajamas next to his Purple Heart.

When he walked the halls
with a lampshade on his head,
cone-shaped privacy screen, they
put him in solitary, upped his dose
of mind-dulling, foot-shuffling pills
and called it a therapeutic milieu.

If you weren't crazy on admission,
you would be by the time you left.

The doctor on call hugged the walls
by day, preferred night's anonymity
when his own demons crawled back
into their dream place— only difference
between staff and patients: the choice
of transcendental medication.

Their chief psychologist had eyes
of steel and West Point hair, kept
a sidekick in his lab coat pocket,
the mean male nurse named Mister
Straight who moonlighted as a cop.

Behind their backs, interns spoke of
gulags, rebelled by sending patients
home, their inner lives in paper bags,
hallucinations now state secrets.

Those were the halcyon days of mental
health: Thorazine shuffle echoing down
halls, electroshock, lobotomies still
weapons of choice— while psychiatrists
wrote papers on the analytic significance
of vacuum cleaners.

Veteran's Affairs

He stands at attention
alone on the median strip
between lanes, posture
parade ground perfect.
Prosthetic leg on the left,
knee brace on the right,
face creased with pain.
Military haircut, his army
shirt torn off at the sleeves,
medals shining like twin
suns on his chest.

In his hands, a frayed
cardboard hand-lettered
sign: *Still standing guard
all these years.* I stop
the car, tearfully empty
my wallet and hand him
what I have. He smiles,
takes my hand and thanks
me for my kindness.
I thank him for his.

The Padded Room

He thought they were taking him
somewhere in an elevator.
Walls padded like someone
moving in or out.

He thought they must have forgotten
something when they walked
him in and left. That they were coming
right back. That they were friends.

He heard the door close behind him
with a click. Inspected the padding,
to protect the furniture, he thought.
A bed, he imagined. A table, a stool.

Where were the buttons to choose
your floor? The red alarm
if the elevator got stuck? Why wasn't
it moving? Where were his friends?

The voices in his head got louder,
nothing to drown them out or remind
him they weren't real. Nothing
to distract him or offer comfort.

You'll be stuck in here forever,
they taunted. *You will never leave.*
There was no one there to tell
him any different.

Where Is Safe?

He couldn't tell the orderly
in faded green scrubs
that the wooden door
to his room was a river,
its grain flowing in rough
waves towards him.
Nor could he say
the walls were glowing
embers blowing
like feathers out the barred
window. That the vinyl floor
was burning.

The orderly with furred claws
told him he'd feel safer
inside this tiny cell of a room.
They wanted him to be a
willing flower, to open softly–
didn't want him to attack them
or harm himself. Tightly curled,
knees to chest on narrow bed,
he made himself the smallest target,
held his breath. Here, he was safe
from demons in the day room– maybe.
But what about the NSA?

Catatonia

She had managed to fly to London
clutching R.D. Laing's, *Knots*– her
last hope. Her world had been reduced
to black and white, confined to two
dimensions. Body rigid, her skin prickled
with fear. She was a petrified forest.

Still as a statue, she stood in the corner
of her bare room for days, facing the wall
or curled into crash pose, arms bracing
thighs, head touching knees, eyes
shutting out the world. No words
for the hell realm she inhabited.

When the ice of her terror melted
just a little, she let me sit beside her.
It took weeks for her to look at me,
longer for her to speak in little more
than a slight breeze. I had to move
closer to listen, had to remain still.

She told me she couldn't hear me
because she wasn't really there.
Not knowing how to answer, I told her
she was loved, that she was safe.
Some days, she let me hold her
for hours until she could finally uncurl.

She called me the Angel from the Void.

Before There Were Pills

Alone on a gray steel bed in a gray room
with no window except in the door,
they said she was a danger to herself.

Postpartum, they called her, melancholy,
depressed– words that didn't touch
her ghostly existence. Only shell

remained, brittle husk expecting nothing.
Electroshock would snap her out of it,
the doctors decided, without asking.

They wanted me (as intern) to watch. To see
her struck by lightning, jolted to her core.
Tied to a gurney, twitching, flopping around

like a dying fish– a dying I would never
forget: a death of the spirit while
the body still lived. Memories gone,

personality all but erased. Docile as a
feather on windless days, she sat waiting
for a spark that would never return.

Fear of the Marketplace

Each night she prayed to a different god
or goddess.   This night the moon
heard her devotions   then cast a spell
with bells of silver,   Selene's radiance.
Her plea was always   the same,
Let me step outside   *the door*
with no hesitation,   *free of terror.*
She was a lightning-struck oak   rooted

to hardwood floors,   branches
reaching only   to the wall.
No bright sky,   no earth touch,
only window light   and the hum
of lamps.   The small, self-
enclosed sanctuary,   a prison.
Each morning   she waited
for the slap   of daily news
on the doorstep,   paper boy
riding off,   neighbor leaving
for work.   Hardly breathing,
she would inch forward,   open the door,

bend down   with curled fingers,
reach around   the frame
to nab her prize.   The relief
of the door   shut   against the world,
followed by   the sour taste of failure.

Alone on the Corner...

She felt the urge to contract
to subatomic anonymity
wrapped in a cocoon
of   mirrors,
invisible.
He
stood
a few feet to
her right listening
to a foreign language
lesson on his phone. He
started to yell at the woman's
voice,   ranted at cars driving by,
then at the man with a beer   in a bag
sitting next to her.   He was an   island,
isolated by insanity.   The bus queue
quietly inched away. Her neighbor asked if she was ok.
She nodded,   not wanting to call attention
to herself,   become another target for his
unfiltered rage.   Where was the bus?
She closed her eyes found the stillness
in her   heart,   began to send
compassion   with her breath.
Wishing she could melt his
agitation, dissolve the
fear pressing blade-
like, sharpening
the   divide
between
them..

Time Out

She was locked in the closet
in her room. No shutters, just
a fingernail of light beneath
the chipped wood door. This time,
she was left there overnight; mom
said she was too awful to let back
in the world. No dinner, no blanket.
No one to soothe her fear.

The only things she could reach
were her shoes lined up like
prisoners on the cracked linoleum
floor. Too dark to see their colors,
she remembered them by shape.
Some had buckles, some laces;
most were twins.

Soon they had names and
complicated stories: the slipper
of a princess, the children
of a queen. She would hold them
in her lap, tell them all her
troubles, sing them to sleep,
steadfast companions.

When the closet door opened,
she cringed, overcome by light,
was told she had better be good.
*Change your clothes, put on
your shoes.* She came out
of the room barefoot, refused
to step on her friends. Soon,
she was back in the closet.

Down the Rabbit Hole

She imagined being Alice eating a mushroom
to make her shrink. Small enough to slip
under the door and into the forest. Or,
maybe big enough to beat the monster
hiding under her bed. She felt jumpy, legs
wiggling, wanted to go out and play.

The room was in shadow, shades down
to keep blue chairs from fading. She was
made to stand in the corner for hours,
facing off-white walls. Ran her fingers up
and down the edges where the walls met,
feeling for cracks where she might escape.

In her mother's eyes, she was the bad one,
her brother, the saint. He couldn't rescue
her or talk to her through the door.
Her crime: getting her school dress dirty,
her new shoes scuffed. Enough time
alone would teach her to be good.

If that didn't work, her dad could be called on
to use his belt. She counted the hours like the white
rabbit. Her mother was the Red Queen.
She wondered if she would starve to death
or be eaten by a caterpillar. She wondered,
would anyone miss her?

Hidden Child

He lived behind a wall in the small attic
Enough space   for dreams of flying
but not enough of an old Dutch house
for small-boy legs to wiggle and   roam
Seated on straw and feathers he would
daydream far off meadows icy streams
where he and his wolf-dog ran   free
in the days before in the   good times
When tired of counting knots and nails
in planks he would conjure   characters
from books his mother had read to him
have long   yet silent   conversations
with imaginary friends   make faces no
one could see   Some days he wore the
mask of *De Moker* his comic book hero
Sometimes   he donned a cloak of fear
The creak of a stair unfamiliar footstep
could end his dreams shatter his   world

Imagining the Bubble Boy

"He never touched the world. But the world was touched by him."
  — From the epitaph for David Vetter (Bubble Boy)

Some, delicate as gossamer cloistering
a world of piety and purpose. Some,
strong as spacecraft windows looking
out on a labyrinth of cosmic stories.

I remember blowing bubbles, wishing
I could ride them to that no one place,
away from raised voices, atomic bomb
drills, threats of polio from swimming pools.

My bubble was a red Hudson Bay blanket.
Beneath it, I could read by flashlight, listen
to music on a tiny radio with ear buds, gift
from my grandma, easy to hide from mom.

I thought everyone lived in their own bubble,
some transparent as jellyfish, others impenetrable.
Riding the trolley car, I used to imagine bubbles touching,
collapsing– souls opening to each other.

Had I known of him then, I probably would have
envied David Vetter, thought he would never get
yelled at or spanked. I'd have imagined him with
everything he desired, prince in his own domain.

Of course, I wouldn't conjure a choiceless life,
couldn't understand the utter restriction or know
his private rage or pain. Most of us can leave our
self-created bubbles without the risk of death.

Locked-in

He awakened, he thought,
from a nightmare
but darkness hung on,
a coarse blanket wrapped
tight around him leaving
little room to breathe.
In his dream, he had crossed
the River Styx with no coin
for Charon nor map for the journey.
There were voices in the distance,
muted, cold. A smell of disinfectant
and dryness, not home. The feel
of much washed, wrinkled linen.
Arms and legs too heavy to lift;
not even his little finger would stir.
Willing movement had no effect.
He was dead wood in a vessel
going nowhere. No one knew
there was someone still in there.
He thought of Alice's Cheshire cat.
Everything gone in the blink
of an eye leaving only an eye blink.

Surviving a SNF*

Renamed Post Acute Care. The last word,
all but invisible– a spurious symbol of
compassion scratched out. His grandmother
is transferred from gurney to bed and left
there alone. Call button dangling, Eve's
apple just out of reach. In the many hours
between drop off and admission,
she might have expired, unnoticed.

A woman finally appears in her room
with a sheaf of papers to be signed. His 100
year-old grandmother reads every line. *What is a DNR,?*
she asks. *Oh, that just means do not resuscitate.*
Oh no, his grandmother says. *I'm not signing that.*
You bring me back. I have too much to live for.
How many sign away their lives without knowing?
How much humiliation awaits the sick, unwary?

Two hours on a bedpan. Backside bared walking
down the hall, hair uncombed. Small requests unheeded:
a cup of water for medication's thirst, an extra towel,
a moment to talk. The impossible wish to sleep through
a night without being poked or measured like a lab rat,
to be seen as more than the heart in 2B.

Where are the healing balms of succor, flowers of relief?
Attentiveness, the rarest jewel, the scent of kindness?
Survival here relies on a coyote's art: part trickster, part cunning,
always vigilant. Knowing when to surrender, when to be fierce.
When to threaten leaving, AMA** or call 911!
His grandmother was a lucky one. She understood bureaucratic
dancing and chose the Paso Doble.

*Skilled Nursing Facility
**Against Medical Advice

Sitting Alone After a Friend's Successful Surgery

Her breath escapes in a
tumbling river at the news.
Who knew it could be held
for centuries, gathering
memories like a hoarder
to ward off catastrophic
fears, those dark, slippery
sewer rats that threaten
equanimity along with
hope, sandpapered
against superstition?

Gratitude. Sky opening
in a downpour of gilded
relief as death brushes
past without stopping,
edging just close enough
for its fetid breath to be
felt and life to become
that much sweeter.

Rendered Invisible

Huddled in the doorway
of a long-closed storefront
with no coat, she ages unnoticed.

Lattes in hand, passersby dressed
in twilight, laugh with ease—
sleepwalk past a life unendurable.

She inhabits an invisible bubble
set apart from life's stream,
untouchable.

Look back at her, really look and you
will turn from stone, from fossil,
see your unadorned reflection

shatter into a thousand pieces—
fragments of a life unlivable.
She resides within you, lone

dweller in shadow, unwatered
seedling, disowned and discarded.
Respect is a homeless woman.

3 QUARANTINE LONELY

A Starry Repast

This one night, quarantine lonely,
I opened the window near my bed
and swallowed the moon. Lit by cool
radiance, perhaps I would embody
lunar wisdom. I wanted to ingest
the Pleiades as well, thought if I
could take within the vastness of
sky dwellers, I would fend off death.

Since everything on earth, including
snow in Antarctica, southwest soil,
my bones (and those of my East
European ancestors) is composed,
in part, of stardust, I would reunite
with far off relations and tap into
infinity. Yet, this insistent yearning

for connection, for eternity, could be
satisfied by even the smallest hermit
crab or blooming hyacinth, bubbling
laugh of a bobolink, the nearness
of my original face. In wanting to eat
the stars, I learned that my hunger
was simply for home.

Opportunity

When I hear rain falling outside my window,
roosters still crowing at two in the afternoon,
I know the world hasn't faded away
and I feel less alone.

Each raindrop is a friend singing softly,
each caw of crow or mating call of coqui,
a message of hope. Nature doesn't want us
to live in despair. Although we've ignored

her warnings, even those gone viral
and acted as if we're the only ones who
matter, Nature will hang in there, battered
or in shreds and show us the mercy of sea

caves, sheltering willows, as she binds
her wounds with plastic bags and fire, once
again reminds us when we're forced to stop
and listen that harmony can be restored.

Going Nowhere in the Time of Covid

One side of the road rimmed in ashes,
the other, pink and yellow blooms.
Ahead, a wild turkey crosses slowly,
somehow knowing there will be no
danger. No cars, no buses, no bicycles.
No one outside or walking. Above, a bevy
of doves on a telephone wire have noticed
something is different.

Around the bend, a lot sits vacant. No
sound but a humming of weeds and stones
revealing what used to be. It is said
the world will be different when this
is over– if it is over. I never used to go
out without earrings, now it's a mask
and gloves. I prefer my adornments
of silver and turquoise.

Nearby, small things catch my attention.
Rain drops have turned a spider's web
into Indra's jeweled net; the frog on a ti
leaf is an opera singer. There is pain
in pausing familiar rhythms, the sacrifice
of intimate gestures, loneliness.
In the time of Covid, sheltering in place
becomes an act of love.

The Gift of Quarantine

The small red flower peering through
a crack in the pavement of my driveway
speaks of miracles. Yesterday, I saw only
imperfection, the need for repair.

Enthralled by the chip in a porcelain cup
rimmed with gold, I run my fingers around
it slowly, thanking rough edges for showing
me the fragility of our world.

With time stretched like a yogi yet moving
faster than a marathon runner, foreground
and background have shifted and once
obscure details are now in sharp focus.

I notice the dust covering well-loved books,
appreciate the shape of a water stain on my counter.
Moonbeams have replaced my mirror, the rising
and setting of planets, my nightly television.

At the end of the day, what I once might have
missed has taken on new luster; my capacity for wonder
has overtaken my need to accomplish. Who knew
quarantine could help restore the soul.

Degrees of Separation

Isolated from ferns, anemones
know not to touch yet commune
across fields of blue-tipped sorrows.

Though tomatoes and marigolds
are ready companions, they keep
their distance to honor human friends.

We are now in exile, expatriates of greed
and excess. A small cup of tea sits in for
a barroom of grieving liqueurs.

Jasmine blooming beside the door:
a jewel in my crown of amazement.
I have clothed myself in book leaves

and online veils. Outside, my mask
and gloves will pass unnoticed. I am
Mata Hari in latex and neoprene.

At war with something invisible:
droplets, aerosols, forbidden words,
Lady MacBeth will have nothing on me.

But is it really war when swans return
to Venice canals, people in China can see
the sun? Despite the pain of quarantine,

I hear the earth rejoicing. What if we stand
with birds and flowers, rivers and trees?
What if we stand for life– and for each other?

Entanglement

Trees branch close together while we
move further apart. They network
and heal each other, converse in leafy
sentences unnoticed by most. For those
fortunate enough to know the language
of quaking aspen and cottonwoods,
there is no separation.

Social distance is the ill-fitting glove
on the hand of Mrs. Malaprop who walks
beside the Grim Reaper on a Florida beach.
For some, sheltering in place equates to
loneliness, wearing masks to lack of freedom.
Yet others find a way to sing to each other
across balconies, share in virtual feasts.

How to measure distance? If our speech
can instantly impact a molecule in a star
at the edge of the universe, how can we
be any less entangled? Our bodies may be
six feet apart or six hundred miles, but if I
think of you, no matter how far away,
you are right there beside me.

In This Time of Transition

Shadows of what once was hover
above unfilled graves, ghosts
of dying stars and paradigms.

Our rhythms and routines, ruptured,
predictability gone. We've been left on
our own in free fall, no ground in view.

Nothing in the world we've counted
on still stands *as is*, old beliefs, habits–
unreliable; we cannot pretend.

We have entered the bardo of becoming,
transitioning from rusted oil rigs, bloat
and toxic cloudburst to what will serve us

better– or disaster. Trees may fruit more
this year or not, roses may be more fragrant
or die before they bloom. Death will show

its funerary mask to many, leave traces
like claw marks on an icy window.
Our hearts will be tenderized, broken.

Yet nature offers us another chance.
There is holiness in grief. Remorse
can realign us to the sacred.

Precious Scars

Black swans call
to their mates
across brackish water

A new language
clear stream
harbored stillness

Heart of the iris
a bee curls inside
my heart fills

This quiet won't easily
give way to shattering
again and again

Fragments of day lilies
interrupted conversations
the dance danced through

Nowhere else to go
but here in this audacious
fragile unfolding newness

Unpause the held breath
exhale starships filled with radiance
the kindness of strangers

Remember to turn ashes
rotting timbers into compost
what germinates will bedazzle

Don't forget why we are:
to love, repair this broken world
the art of kintsugi*

*Japanese art of repairing broken pottery with seams of gold, adding to its beauty and strength

Quarantine's Root

Forty days, the root of quarantine.
Time enough to plant a forest,
find your shadow in pain's desert.

Time for contemplation, ceiling gazing,
climbing walls. Time enough to feel
collective terror, yearning.

For those without a roof, place to wash
or keep their distance, there is no time.
Standing on the street or in a corner,

tears stream down life-lined faces as hands
reach out for something, anything. A heartfelt
blessing follows that dollar bill you offer,

a wind that lifts your sails and speeds you home
to shelter back in place where you stay rooted
in unknowing. And think of loss while waiting

out this science fiction drama. Loss of touch,
vital to the heart as blood, loss of easy gathering.
Absent any givens, we can surely get lost.

Forty days or more of less than comfortable
uncertainty. Unless we find a way to take
our comfort in the groundless.

The Walls

in a house
a measure of sanity
or strength of habit

When they seem
to float
and the world
is less solid

nothing to hold on to
nothing to reject

beauty steps in
to fill any cracks
and zinnias bloom
in the living room

When they shimmer
with dreams of star-
struck spirit
mythology reigns
and queens are born

When they seem
to move in
and grow closer

fear has sprung a leak
in the body electric
set teeth abuzz
solar plexus humming

And when they grow
further away
more transparent
I know I have
lost my mind

a spacious moment
deliriously free

The Weight of Loss

Loss can be measured
against the heaviness
of rain, stones tumbling
into brook and fire,
the cry of a newborn,
silence of the stillborn.
What can you deduct
from zero?

When there are too many
losses to count or bear, list
what you can be grateful for:
sun warming grief-wracked
hands, the smile of a drifter
wanting nothing in return,
an old photograph
reminding you of love.

When you have nothing else—
burn a candle, light the stove,
pick a yellow flower,
a blooming weed to place
in a glass, perfume your bath
with children's stories
and rosemary. Find sanctity,
take comfort in the breath.

What Will Carry Us Through

I'd like to offer you
the stars at dusk,
that brief but
memorable twinkle
in the eyes of the Divine,
that green flash
at sunset,
a murmuration of starlings.

It doesn't matter
if these wishes
remain virtual
or that I cannot
bring you
a glass of wine
or cook you a meal.
Doesn't even matter
if we haven't spoken.

What will carry us
through and sustain us:
the language and splendor
of the heart, that
rare, perennial flower,
always present,
always accessible,
no matter how
isolated we are.

Where is Here?

In this time of maximum uncertainty,
gardenia petals drop to the grass, filling
the air with unsurprising sweetness
that counters the sour taste of fear.

Though we can always find reasons to doubt
the truth of constellations or seasons, we can
also uncover beauty in the most obscure
places without questioning why.

The need to know, to control the flow
of gravity, build an altar to permanence filled
with phantoms, will crumble in the face of
the real, the transient– leaving ashes and crumbs

too small to matter. Better to move beyond
the circle of a wishful *not here* to *what is*
and then imagine *what could be,*
knowing it is only a dream.
Just for fun, I have named each room in my house

a different city and travel by foot from place
to place. With Rome as my living room,
Paris my kitchen, I will sleep in Hawaii, write
poetry in Madrid without leaving home.

What Comes Next

Like origami unfolded, then refolded slowly
into something new– or the settling of tea

leaves in a stoneware cup, the future is a
mystery read mostly by prophets.

When the quarantine is over, will we forget
the cactus on a windowsill near our bed,

hazy, sunlit strolls around the block when
no one's out? Will we forget our loneliness,

our yearning for each other when we couldn't
see each other, when even the thought of

touching was enough to think of death? Will
we remember waking with the slow but certain

knowledge we're alive, we're still alive! Or the
simple joy of slowing down and noticing?

We've had the time to notice: fragments of
reflections on a faucet, geckoes slowly climbing

on a branch outside the door, all the books
we haven't looked at, how little we get by with,

how little we really need. Will we recall the days
of dread, no roses– when there was nothing to

distract or reassure us that the future would be
better than the past? Won't matter, if only we can

live without regret and rise above each tremor,
every heartache. If we hold steady, grateful,

open-hearted as the world begins to reassemble,
our smallest contributions will bear fruit.

4 BLESSED SOLITUDE

A Forest Ranger's Prayer

A limestone cave: my church.
The nearby stream and blueberry
bushes– where I take communion.

A choir of crickets accompanies
the unseen dove in a pine tree
who offers a sermon on devotion.

Though the tag reads forest ranger
beneath my name, I am a supplicant
in this wilderness temple.

Nature is my sanctuary– the forest,
a living prayer, bears and squirrels,
my fellow parishioners. Here, humans

are rare and no discordant noises
punctuate the silence. Here, only
natural harmonies prevail; my work,

a catalogue of astonishment. A raven
reminds me to stay humble. In this
blessed solitude, I am never lonely.

The Fire Lookout

It began as a lark, a dare born of boredom,
summer fling to a far flung forest at the edge
of my world that morphed into love of the unruly.

At first I was restless, lonely– looking out at forbidding
masses of jade and shadow that seemed to edge closer
as day waned, a uniformity that staggered me,

promised to upend all sense of self. I couldn't see
the gloved hands of trees for the forest, adrift as I was
on waves of monotony, a sleep of the unawakened.

Each night was a slow dragon whose tail wrapped around
my breath, my eyes half open, afraid the vastness would
defeat me, mirror how flimsy my anchors to reality.

Then a heat spell when lightning struck, parted the veils as
wisps of smoke, then fire grabbed my attention. I was electrified:
awareness, now a panorama of vivid detail, infinite shading.

That first call, an initiation. Nature had claimed me,
recalled my debt to earthy origins, married me
to the pulse of the world. Solitude became my brother.

Kate's Light

Mind the light, Kate,
her husband's last words,
ballast for a widow's work.
When I first came to Robbins
Reef Light Station, the sight
of the water, whichever way
I looked, made me lonesome.

Home: a cast iron cylinder
on a tiny rock islet in New York
harbor. At first, she wanted to leave;
her future seemed bleak as the Stygian
depths. But she persevered, the fate
of ships and their sailors soon
steady as a foghorn in her hands.

The light, tended from sunset 'til dawn:
lamps refilled, clockwork for the lens
rewound, siren maintained for foggy
weather to protect those ghosts
in the night. Fifty sailors, over thirty
years, saved by this petite, yet sturdy
lighthouse keeper.

Too busy to be lonely, she came
to fear going ashore, leaving only
to row her children to a Staten Island
school. Isolation only strengthened
her resolve. She was a true light
in the harbor, guardian of safe
passage on storm-ridden seas.

Long Haul Trucker

Windows open, a brisk wind
sings me down unending asphalt
bordered on one side by river,
the other by juniper and sage.
Small desert towns rush past,
a mirage of civilization.

The open road at 5 a.m. when
night meets morning as a tired
lover and the only sounds are
shifting gears and rolling tires.
My favorite time: the CB radio
off, my handle, *Night Dog*, silent–

at one with my rig and the road.
No other life has worked for me,
not building houses or sitting in
an office nine to five. A solitary
trucker, the call of the highway
sweetens my blood.

Night Janitor

Keeper of secrets, his job
begins once the sun has
disappeared and night has
settled in with its caravan
of stars.

Trash baskets harbor
treasure; he empties them
with care, not knowing
what he may find: torn love
letters, an old photo reduced
to ash, a single gold earring.

Ghostly imprints of those
who left for home remain
like indentations on a note
pad. Unseen, he wanders
long halls, mop and broom
his only companions, just
the way he likes it.

The Art of Solitude

If someone approaches you and asks
if you want company, say no.

You don't have to be an island
free of greening shores or empty
your cupboards; you can take
down *No Trespassing* signs
outside your bedroom window.

There's no need to turn off
your phone or stop the mail.
Missionaries will forget to call
once they know you've given up
religion for the new year.

You can tell people you're gone
for the winter; the person
they see buying chamomile tea
at the grocery store must be
a long lost relative.

It's easier if you stay at home—
no doppelgangers to worry about.
In a crowd, you can always claim
stolen identity or that ear buds playing
no music make it hard for you to hear.

You can also look lost, stranger
in unfamiliar territory, student
of beginner's mind. Then, it won't
matter, alone or not, your time
will be worth something.

There Are Days

when solitude is not my friend, not
the sought after respite from a mad
world or retreat of renunciates
seeking enlightenment, not the
sanctuary of ferns and marsh.

Today, my sense of isolation hangs
heavy as a twisted trumpet vine,
endless woody stem poking holes
in weakened stucco, an unwelcome
grief. To cheer myself, I will fill

the house with music, invite in
anyone who wants to visit,
remember I'm not really alone.
Today, I need that. Birdsong and
chrysanthemums are not enough.

But tomorrow, I will build a shrine
to loneliness, place carefully chosen
stones and crystals near a vase of
dried statis, a Navajo storyteller doll
with her many children, beloved

photos, a bowl of sweet figs and
pomegranates to feed and honor
those darker feelings of lack– until I
can once again recall the abundance,
the sacredness of solitude.

Lucid Dreaming

In the sanctuary of dreams
when night swoons
over a lilting moon and owls
question dark's embrace,
I am content to be alone.
In this landscape of sleep,
I am conjurer and vessel.

My mind has summoned
a pastoral scene, unpeopled,
sought refuge in frangipani
and filaree, in the soft
underbelly of mosses and
marigolds, in the silence
of stars.

Under a fairytale moon
whose light ruffles leaves
and leaves a trail of watery
tears, I dance with abandon,
dance out my sorrow, dance
away fear.

The safety of willow boughs,
trill of sparrow song fill me
with peace. Staying aware,
I can move from dreamscape
to waking life and know
there is no real difference.

Walking the Path Alone

One day I gathered courage
like a summer wind, tuned
out the doubts, familiar strains
that held me back
and bound me
feet first
to the same dead places,
ignored the plaintive calls
to not think
only of myself
and took those first few steps
beyond the walls,
beyond the terrible magnetic pull
of all that went before–
the hymns of uncertainty,
the fear
that called me back
and filled the path
with gullies and boulders.
I stumbled alone
through
the moonless night
alive with unknown
voices; the rise and fall
of my breath
kept pace
with lengthening footfalls.
Slowly my thoughts
shook off habitual cocoons,
mirrored
each fresh moment
unencumbered
as I recognized
what I was meant to do.
Distance brought strength,
the lights of fireflies
soft comfort–
and the certainty
I would never turn back.

Solitude

Solitude draped like a cloak,
renders me invisible to distraction,
shelters me from ragged political
currents and uncertain weather.

I can hide within it, from myself
and the world– or open in a way
that doesn't disturb my solitude yet
includes everything. All I need is to

let go of judgments and assumptions.
Much of what I think I know is what
I think; thoughts replace the sky,
the gift of snow geese flying,

the untrammeled view of an eagle.
There are so many blessings in watching
the birth of a foal from my window—
no words, no concepts, just joy.

Isn't It Something

how even a single
fallen leaf can bring
you back into life
when you feel
most disconnected,
how its crisp curled
edges, its brittle rust
and brown body,
the way it rests
on a lichen-covered
rock can call you
to that hallowed space
of awe?

Isn't it something
how the song of a
cardinal on the high
branch of an elm
tree can remind you
of the absence of a
loved one, how its
sweet notes can lift
you beyond grief
and despair?

Isn't it something
how the drawing
down of night dark
with the shimmer
of cloud-shadowed
moon gently
dusting the trees
is enough to lighten
the weight of solitary
introspection, to
deepen initiatory
dreams?

Advantages of Solitude

a swan among seagulls
the lift of wind on a wing
the beauty of a solitary star
take me with you

some thrive on solitude
an unfolding of freedom
in the heart of moonflower
alone amid so many asterisms

in the vastness of sky
so many heartbeats
no one else can hear
the virtue of an empty room

so easy to commune with butterflies
listen to the music of palm fronds
or sit with a loveliness of ladybugs
in the council of silence

so joyful to relax in stillness
time to do nothing be nothing
a quiet evening
with only lunar reflections

Kuchisabishi: Eating Because My Mouth Is Lonely

Below the tree line, I reach
for a word to reflect the deep
love of nature that fills me while
alone in the forest or at the ocean
but there's nothing in English that's
close to what I feel; words like

waldeinsamkeit: the deep peace
of being connected to nature when
alone or *yuugen*: profound grace
and awareness of the oneness of all
things. Or *wabi sabi*: finding beauty
in imperfection, impermanence.

How differently we might view the
world if we had such words– letters
carefully strung together as a necklace
of insight and wisdom, immeasurable
joy in subtle hues: lifeline for the tender,
inexpressible.

Pay Attention

The coconut palm behind
my left shoulder whispers
in my ear, *Pay attention,*
there is no one here. I pause
at a bowl-shaped lava rock
and look towards the sea.
At first I notice people walking,
birds scavenging, waves
dancing with dolphins and clouds.
In the tidal pool, tiny fish
and hermit crabs exchange
simple greetings.

A whirl of energy and motion, yet
underneath, profound stillness
and peace. When I let myself
sink into this all-pervasive, lively
space, the universe of separate
things dissolves into a collage
of color and sound, shapes
unlabeled, passing thoughts.
Nothing stands out or stands
apart. Everything is background
to this sparkling, open presence—
awareness with no one present.

5 LETTING GO OF THE WORLD

Hagiography

When I need to nourish
my faltering spirit
I look to the lives
of mystics and saints

in caves
in cells
or mountain abodes

like tea lights
         scattered
                 along
                     old church
                           walls
fireflies
       in a forest
               of sorrows

Alone
with thoughts
prolific as rabbits
realization
a still fragile bloom
they fill their days
with prayers and practice
with noble aspirations
to fully awaken

Letting go of the world
they meditate on love
offer their blessings
          to illuminate
               the way

The Problem for Some with Renunciation

As spiritual devotee,
you give away
your belongings—
a grand gesture
with sincere intent,
renounce the world
and retreat to a cave
with no distractions.
You aspire to dwell
wholly in the Divine.
But somehow, the world
follows you, thoughts
crowd your inner space
competing with each
other, repeat themselves,
drown out the roar of
nearby river. Feelings
long disowned demand
attention like unruly
children. You question
why you sit in isolation
when everything you
left behind is still there
with you. No possessions
yet still possessed.

If Wishes Were Golden

It takes more than a wish to awaken
for the benefit of others and oneself.
You have to want it more than
breath itself, more than moonlit
pleasures or seasonal comforts.

You must be willing to let go
of all you think you know, your
worldly concerns and signs of
status. You have to become a
nobody, stripped of ego

adornments, yearning to rest in
pure awareness. In solitary retreat
with no outer distractions, you may
start to open, feel more spacious,
thoughts and feelings moving to

background yet nothing excluded.
Herein lies your essence: awake
and unimpeded, inseparable from
all that is— a radiance of wisdom
and compassion awaiting recognition.

Christ Has No Body
Teresa of Avila

And if you enter her room   while
she is at vespers   and if you lean
against the wall,   you will feel
bare planks   imbued with
the perfumed resin   of prayer,
cracks filled in   with piety
and purity of purpose.   And the
barely audible hum   of continual,
ecstatic devotion. Gravity has fled
this windowless cell,   this aerie of
a wingless bird. There are no flight
restrictions,   no limits to soaring.
A subtle lightreveals the   Sacred.
No crucifix   is needed.

From Seductress to Saint: Maria Aegyptiaca

A life of insatiable lust, seeking men like homing pigeons
seek home, she offers sexual favors for passage to Jerusalem.

Turned away three times from Church of the Holy Sepulcher
by an unseen force, the closed door sparks her salvation.

Remorse, like soured milk, fills her impure vessel
imploring her to leave her life of debauchery and sin.

Before a statue of the Virgin with arms outstretched, a
welcoming angel, Maria weeps and prays for forgiveness.

Promises to renounce all desire, give up the world.
This time, the church opens– she sees the True Cross.

On fire with gratitude following conversion, she hears a
voice, *If you cross the Jordan River, you'll find glorious rest.*

Crossing the river with only three loaves of bread, she
repudiates the darkness and turns toward the light.

Through 17 years of trials and base temptations, the desert
wilderness has become her sanctuary. Her faith in God,

unshakable as granite, sustains her naked in a life of prayer
and penance. After 47 solitary years, in a chance encounter,

she tells her story to St. Zosimas. Sanctified, she walks on water
across the Jordan for Holy Communion. She asks him to meet her

the following Lent. Yet death awaits; found the next year, her incorrupt
body returned to the place they first met. An inscription in the sand reads,

She died immediately after receiving communion. Buried by Zosimas
with the help of a lion, she was a true Desert Mother* and saint.

*Christian ascetics living in the desert of Egypt, Palestine, and Syria in the 4th and 5th
centuries AD

Julian of Norwich, Anchoress*
"And all shall be well and every kind of thing shall be well for there is a force of love moving through the-universe that holds us fast and will never let us go."
    –From Revelations of Divine Love.

Three days
deathly ill
Last rites
Curate with
a crucifix
at the foot
of her bed
What sickness
has wrought:
Jesus bleeding
a darkening
numbness
sixteen
visions
of Christ

Recovery:
Sealed into
a tomblike cell
attached to
St. Julian's church
Funeral psalms
sung for her
Now dead
to the world
to the ordinary
but alive and
devoted to God
to solitary prayer

Revelations
of Divine Love:
For He that made man
for the sake of love, would
by the same love
restore man to bliss,
even greater than before

*anchoress: woman who withdraws from the world for solitary life of prayer/contemplation

Milarepa

A Buddhist lama once said, *If you do
nothing else, purify your intentions.*

What if you've murdered people,
using black magic to avenge your family,
can you still become enlightened? After
Milarepa, Tibet's great yogi, committed

such terrible acts, he was overcome
with remorse. His sleep was haunted,
regret filled every waking moment,
grief stalked his nights.

He sought out a spiritual teacher
wanting salvation. To purify his negative
karma, Marpa had him build and rebuild
stone towers for years, followed by

dharma teachings, decades of meditation
alone in a cave. There, he faced inner
demons, outer privation– naked, green
from his diet of nettle soup. Then, finally,

awakening, the precious jewel of realizing
one's true nature– awareness vast as sky,
luminous and unobstructed. The bliss of
resting in mind's essence with compassion,

loving kindness for all. Stories of miracles
followed: flying, melting snow with inner heat,
songs of realization and, most important–
leading others to enlightenment.

Twelve Years in Solitary Retreat

*"What people have to remember is that meditators in caves are not doing it for themselves—
they're meditating on behalf of all sentient beings."*

– Ani Tenzin Palmo

The snow is a blanket covering doubt,
binding the retreatant to her inner life.
Alone at 13,000 feet, no need for social
gestures, for habits of conformity.

Silence is a welcome home, the music
of the Absolute. The cave, a comforting
fortress of humility, determination. No
hardship too hard to endure when you

know you're in the right place, when the
vow to reach enlightenment in the body
of a woman fuels your resolve, makes
light of any obstacle. Sleep becomes

unnecessary as subtler levels of
consciousness revealed by meditation
refresh the body and mind. For Tenzin
Palmo, solitude was never lonely, fear—

an absent stranger. Twelve years in
retreat flew by in timelessness,
imbued with states of inner joy, of
knowing without the knower.

To my mind the contemplatives and the
solitary meditators are like lighthouses
beaming out love and compassion on to
the world.*

* Ani Tenzin Palmo. Mackenzie, Vicki. *Cave In The Snow* (p. 196). Bloomsbury Publishing.
Kindle Edition.

Seeking Sanctuary

Fleeing violence in one form
only to find it in another:
indifference, intolerance,
inhumanity.

Seeking a safe haven.

The church doors,
welcoming arms—
invite trust, offer
protection.

A place to rest
where dreams return
as far off possibilities,
unarticulated.

The outer world,
stranger on sabbatical.

Settling into sanctuary,
bittersweet respite
from chaos.
Fears set aside like
so many old newspapers—
their headlines

faint but still visible:
Deportation on the Horizon;
Reality Just Outside the Door.
Soon solitude turns
on its heel

leaves loneliness in its stead.
Mourning separation
from family, from culture—
future freedom in question.

Yet, grateful for this refuge,
the kindness of strangers,
hope flutters in dark corners
lifting despair.

Priest Holes

"Goosey Goosey Gander where shall I wander,
Upstairs, downstairs and in my lady's chamber
There I met an old man who wouldn't say his prayers,
I took him by the left leg and threw him down the stairs."

    – 16th century English nursery rhyme

"Off with their heads."

    –The Red Queen, Alice in Wonderland

Fear permeates stone walls of an old
Tudor mansion, unrelieved by wealth
or stature, the presence of nobles. Here,
celebrations of Mass, of faith demand
hidden rites and secret chambers.

What can be concealed in a fetid,
airless, tiny room behind a fireplace
under the floor? Prayers in Latin
instead of English, a silver chalice,
a beloved hymnal.

Protestant priest hunters, their quarry,
Catholic clergy– measure walls
for discrepancies, pull up floorboards
in their awful quest, pretend to leave
then lie in wait. The built-in hideout,

poor refuge for the traveling priest.
Though cramped, starving, afraid of
discovery, he prays the Rosary while
he ponders Last Rites. Capture, torture,
hanging or beheading– his likely fate.

Refuge From Shame

A woman in medieval England,
strong as willow with the healing
touch of borage and boneset, her
wit and tongue, sharp scissors—

might have been given two choices:
don the mask of shame, scolder's
bridle, or seek sanctuary in a church.
Nagging her husband, gossiping,

too much curiosity or hints of
witchcraft were enough to put her
in an iron mask with a gag and spike
to pierce the tongue so she couldn't

eat or speak for days while paraded
through the streets for maximum
humiliation and punishment.
She might have sought out

sanctuary instead— from a controlling
husband, tattletale neighbors, envious
friends. She might have chosen
God over man.

Juana Dreams of Unconfined Spaces

A thousand pillows sewn
with tiny stitches by Guatemalan
hands– for others to rest
their heads. A way to fend off
boredom, keep her fears at bay.

At night, she dreams of family
reunions, unconfined spaces–
freedom to go anywhere or nowhere.
A life without borders or patrols.
She prays for the blessing

of a work permit or, best of all, full
citizenship. Her recurrent nightmare,
an ICE agent breaking through the old
church door: deportation, death. For
two decades, Juana stitched her way

to security in America until a raid
threatened her with expulsion. After
several long years claiming sanctuary
in a small room in a church, will she
end up sewing comforters or shrouds?

To Find Sanctuary in This World

first sanctify the mind,
orient it toward the sacred;
purify those swirling clouds
of negativity– those thoughts
and feelings of fear or despair
that rise and fall away like
so many autumn leaves in
wind. At any moment, you can
let them be as if watching
a movie of no interest.
You can also see through them
to the stillness and compassion–
the true sanctuary that lies within.

Make the ordinary holy with
reverence and respect. Make
washing dishes, sweeping floors
a sacrament conferring grace.
Anything done with presence,
full attention brings forth the
luminosity of spirit. You never
know what form an angel or
bodhisattva will assume, never
know what gifts there are– at a
laundromat or waiting for a train.

Find beauty in imperfection,
in the most unlikely places,
even in darkest times: the glitter
of an old tin can in sunlight,
cry of a vulture sweeping down
for its evening meal, the lone
flower on a child's grave.
Seek solitude in nature,
the solace of starlings
and sycamores.

ACKNOWLEDGMENTS

In Memory of Herman Wallace was published in *Rise Up Review*.

A Chance for Salvation was published in *Valiant Scribe Literary Journal* and was nominated for Best of the Net, 2025.

Christ Has No Body appeared in *Young Ravens*.

Where is Here was published in *Dreams walking*.

Going Nowhere in the Time of Covid appeared on WNYC: lessons learned.

The Redemption of Maria Aegyptiaca (St. Mary of Egypt) was published in *Agape Review*.

The following poems: A Starry Repast, Opportunity, Going Nowhere in the Time of Covid, The Gift of Quarantine, Degrees of Separation, Entanglement, In This Time of Transition, Precious Scars, Quarantine's Root, The Walls, The Weight of Loss, What Will Carry us Through, Where is Here?, What Comes Next appeared in *Going Nowhere in the Time of Corona*, published online by issuu.com.

ABOUT THE AUTHOR

Carol Alena Aronoff, Ph.D. is a psychologist, teacher and writer who co-founded SAGE, a psycho-spiritual program for elders; helped guide a Tibetan Buddhist Meditation center for seven years; taught Eastern spirituality, health and meditation practices; imagery in healing; and women's health at San Francisco State University for nearly 14 years. She guided Healing in Nature retreats in Hawaii and the Southwest, had a counseling practice in Marin for many years. She co-authored *Practical Buddhism: The Kagyu Path* with Ole Nydah, 1989 and edited five books and four meditation booklets on Tibetan Buddhism. Dr. Aronoff published a textbook: *Compassionate Healing: Eastern Perspectives* in 1992.

Her poetry has been published in more than 100 literary journals including *Comstock Re-view, Poetic Realm, Poetica, Heart Lodge, Buckle &, Sendero, Iodine, Asphodel, Nomad's Choir, Cyclamens & Swords, The New Verse News, Quill & Parchment, Verse-Virtual, Avocet., Bosque, Sourland Review, Vox Poetica, Panoplyzine, Amethyst Review, Total Eclipse, Foreign Literary Journal,* et al. Her poems also appear in anthologies such as *Out of Line, 200 New Mexico Poems, Women Write Resistance, Before There is Nowhere to Stand, Malala, Poetry of the American Southwest, Dove Tales: Empathy in Art: Em-bracing the Other* and *You Can Hear the Ocean: An Anthology of Classic and Current Poetry.*

She received a prize in the 1999/2000 Common Ground spiritual poetry contest, judged by Jane Hirshfield and was twice a Pushcart Prize nominee. She won the Tiger's Eye contest on the writing life, participated a number of times in *Braided Lives, A Collaboration Between Artists and Poets* as well as in SKEA's Art & Nature event; *Ekphrasis: Sacred Stories of the Southwest* and (A) *Muses Poster Retrospective*, Taos. She judged the 2008 Tiger's Eye poetry contest.

A chapbook of Native American/Hawaiian poems, *Cornsilk*, was published by Indian Heritage Council in 2004 and her illustrated poetry book, *The Nature of Music*, was published by Pelican Pond/Blue Dolphin Publishing in 2005. An expanded, illustrated *Cornsilk* was published in 2006, *Her Soup Made the Moon Weep,* in 2007 and *Blessings from an Unseen World* in 2013. *Dreaming Earth's Body* with paintings by Betsie Miller-Kusz was published in 2015. The poetry collection, *Tapestry of Secrets*, was published by Finishing Line Press in 2019 and was a finalist for the New Mexico/ Arizona Book Awards in 2020. A chapbook of pandemic poetry, *Going Nowhere in the Time of Corona* was self-published online in 2020 at issuu.com. *The Gift of Not Finding: Poems for Meditation* was published by Homestead Lighthouse Press in 2020. *A Time to Listen* was published in 2023.

Currently, Carol resides in a rural area of Hawaii, meditating in nature and writing.